ETHICAL ENLIGHTENMENT

A MODERN GUIDE TO LIVING WITH INTEGRITY

DR. MINAKSHI BANSAL

Dedicated to all those who strive for a world where integrity, compassion, and justice prevail. May your unwavering commitment to ethical living inspire others to follow in your footsteps, and may your actions serve as a beacon of hope in a world that often feels fraught with moral uncertainty. This book is dedicated to you—the champions of ethical enlightenment—who remind us that even in the face of adversity, goodness and decency can prevail.

Contents

Contents

Contents

Prayer

"Om Bhadram Karnebhih Shrinuyama Devah
Bhadram Pashyemakshabhiryajatrah
Sthirairangais Tushtuvamsastanubhih
Vyashema Devahitam Yadayuh
Svasti Na Indro Vriddhashravah
Svasti Nah Pusha Vishwavedah
Svasti Nastarkshyo Arishtanemih
Svasti No Brihaspatir Dadhatu
Om Shantih Shantih Shantih"

This mantra is a prayer for universal well-being, invoking the blessings of various deities for protection, health, and happiness. It emphasizes the importance of experiencing the auspicious through all senses and living a life aligned with divine purpose. The repetition of "Shantih" at the end signifies a deep desire for peace in the individual, the environment, and the universe at large. This mantra is often recited as a prayer for peace, prosperity, and the physical and spiritual well-being of all beings.

About The Author

Dr. Minakshi Bansal, born in the bustling metropolis of Delhi, India, has led a life steeped in artistry, scholarly pursuit, and an unwavering commitment to societal betterment. Following her marriage, she relocated to Ahmedabad, Gujarat, where she has since blossomed into a multifaceted beacon of inspiration for many. Dr. Minakshi is not only recognized as a gifted artist in the realm of Fine Arts but also as an esteemed author, a devoted social worker and a dedicated research scholar in Psychology. Her journey, marked by a profound dedication to elevating those around her, especially the downtrodden and underprivileged children of society, is a testament to her deep-seated belief in the transformative power of engagement and empathy.

From her earliest days, Minakshi was distinguished by an insatiable appetite for reading. Her literary universe was inhabited by characters and narratives that spanned ethical tales, motivational and inspirational stories, and the mythic parables imbued with life lessons. This voracious reading habit was not merely for personal edification but was driven by a desire to distill and disseminate the essence of these narratives to foster the development of students and peers alike. She was particularly captivated by the lives and teachings of historical figures and spiritual leaders such as Adi Shankaracharya, Swami Vivekananda, Dr. APJ Abdul Kalam, Mahamana Pandit Madan Mohan Malviya, Mahatma Gandhi, Sardar Vallabhai Patel, and Vinoba Bhave, among others. Their philosophies and life stories fueled her ambition to embody their ideals of resilience, selflessness, and relentless pursuit of knowledge.

Dr. Minakshi's academic and practical engagement with psychology has been equally noteworthy. As a research scholar, her focus has been on exploring the intricate tapestry of the human psyche, aiming to unlock the potential for psychological well-being and societal harmony. Her scholarly work is complemented by her active involvement in social work, where she employs her academic insights to make tangible differences in the lives of the underprivileged. Her endeavours in social work are characterized by an innovative approach that combines traditional wisdom with contemporary psychological practices to address the multifaceted challenges faced by these communities.

Her artistic talents, another facet of her diverse capabilities, are not merely a personal passion but also serve as a medium through which she communicates and connects with others. Her art, rich in symbolism and emotional depth, reflects her philosophical inquiries and social concerns, offering viewers a glimpse into the breadth of her intellect and the depth of her compassion.

In addition to her contributions to the arts and social sciences, Dr. Minakshi has embraced the healing arts of Pranic Healing, mastering the techniques developed by Master Choa Kok Sui. This practice, which focuses on the manipulation of Prana or life energy to heal the body and aura, has been both a personal journey of discovery and a means through which she extends her healing touch to others. Her proficiency in Pranic Healing is complemented by her advocacy and teaching of various forms of meditation aimed at rejuvenation, personal betterment, and the cultivation of harmony within individuals and communities alike.

Dr. Minakshi's life is a narrative of relentless pursuit, not just of personal achievement but of the upliftment and empowerment of society at large. Her diverse interests and talents—spanning the arts, literature, psychology, and the healing practices—converge on a singular path of service. She embodies the spirit of the luminaries who inspired her, channelling their legacy through her actions and teachings. Through her books, art, and social initiatives, she continues to inspire a new generation to embark on their own journeys of self-discovery, resilience, and altruism.

Her commitment to social betterment, particularly her focus on uplifting underprivileged children, reflects a deep understanding of the transformative potential of education and personal development. By integrating her knowledge of psychology, her artistic sensibilities, and her healing practices, Dr. Bansal has developed a holistic approach to social work that addresses both the immediate needs and the long-term well-being of the communities she serves.

As an author, Dr. Minakshi's writings offer a blend of inspirational insights, practical wisdom, and reflective contemplations drawn from her extensive reading and life experiences. Her books serve as a guide for those seeking to navigate the complexities of life with grace, resilience, and purpose. Through her narratives, she extends an invitation to her readers to explore the depths of their own potential and to contribute meaningfully to the collective well-being of society.

In Dr. Minakshi Bansal, we find a remarkable synthesis of the artist, the scholar, the healer, and the social activist. Her life's work stands as a beacon of hope and a source of inspiration for individuals seeking to make a difference in the world. Her story is a compelling reminder of the power of individual action, rooted in compassion and driven by a profound commitment to the betterment of humanity. Dr. Minakshi's legacy is not just in the tangible outcomes of her efforts but in the enduring spirit of inquiry, empathy, and service that she embodies.

Preface

As I sit down to write this preface for "Ethical Enlightenment: A Modern Guide to Living with Integrity," I am filled with a sense of purpose and responsibility. This book is the culmination of years of reflection, research, and personal experience, and it is my sincere hope that it will serve as a valuable resource for readers seeking to navigate the complexities of ethical living in the modern world.

Ethics has always been a subject close to my heart. From a young age, I was taught the importance of honesty, kindness, and fairness in all my interactions. As I grew older and encountered the myriad ethical dilemmas that life presents, I found myself grappling with questions of right and wrong, seeking guidance from philosophers, religious teachings, and the wisdom of those around me.

The idea for this book emerged from my own journey towards ethical enlightenment—a journey marked by moments of clarity, confusion, and growth. I realized that while there are many books on ethics available, few offer practical guidance for applying ethical principles to the complexities of everyday life. It is my hope that "Ethical Enlightenment" fills this gap, providing readers with tools, insights, and inspiration to live with integrity in a world fraught with moral ambiguity.

Throughout the pages of this book, I draw upon a diverse range of sources, from ancient philosophical texts to contemporary case studies, to illustrate key concepts and principles. I believe that ethics is a dynamic and evolving field, shaped by the cultural, social, and technological changes of our time. As such, "Ethical Enlightenment" reflects a modern perspective on ethics—one that is inclusive, adaptive, and responsive to the challenges of our rapidly changing world.

One of the central themes of this book is the importance of empathy—the ability to understand and share the feelings of others—in guiding ethical behavior. I firmly believe that empathy lies at the heart of all ethical decision-making, enabling us to consider the perspectives and needs of those around us and to act with compassion and integrity.

Another key aspect of "Ethical Enlightenment" is its emphasis on personal responsibility. Ethics is not something that exists in the abstract realm of theory; it is a lived experience, shaped by the choices we make and the actions we take. Each of us has a role to play in creating a more ethical world, and it is my hope that this book will empower readers to embrace that responsibility with courage and conviction.

In writing this book, I have sought to strike a balance between theory and practice, philosophy and real-world application. Each chapter begins with an exploration of key ethical concepts and principles, followed by practical strategies and exercises to help readers apply these principles to their own lives. Whether you are grappling with ethical dilemmas in the workplace, navigating complex relationships, or seeking to make a positive impact on the world, I hope that you will find something of value in these pages.

I am deeply grateful to all those who have supported me in the writing of this book—friends, family, colleagues, and mentors who have offered encouragement, feedback, and inspiration along the way. I am also grateful to the countless individuals whose stories and experiences have enriched my understanding of ethics and deepened my commitment to living with integrity.

As I send this book out into the world, I do so with humility and gratitude, knowing that it is only through the collective efforts of all those who strive for ethical enlightenment that we can truly create a more just, compassionate, and sustainable world. May "Ethical

Enlightenment" serve as a guide and companion on your own journey towards living with integrity, and may it inspire you to embrace the power of ethical living to transform yourself and the world around you.

With warmest wishes,

Dr. Minakshi Bansal
Social Activist
Ahmedabad, Gujarat, Bharat

The Foundation of Integrity: Understanding Core Ethical Values

Integrity is a quality that has long been admired in individuals across all cultures and ages. It stands as the bedrock of character, the essence of how we conduct ourselves in the world.

Integrity is often associated with honesty, but it encompasses much more. It involves being true to yourself, keeping your promises, and living by the principles you believe to be right, even when no one is watching. At its core, integrity is about consistency between what we say and what we do, as well as between our values and our actions.

To develop integrity, one must first understand the core ethical values that underpin it. These values serve as a compass that guides us through life's challenges and dilemmas. Some of the key ethical values include honesty, respect, responsibility, fairness, and compassion. Each of these plays a vital role in shaping a person of integrity.

Honesty is the foundation of integrity and involves telling the truth, being open, and avoiding deceit or fraud. Honest individuals are trustworthy, reliable, and sincere. They do not distort facts for personal gain and are straightforward in their dealings with others. Honesty builds trust, and trust is crucial for sustaining any meaningful relationship, whether personal or professional.

Respect is another critical ethical value. It means recognizing the worth and dignity of every person, regardless of their status or disagreements you may have with them. Respect involves listening to others, valuing their opinions, and treating them with courtesy. In a world as diverse as ours, respect for others is essential for peaceful coexistence and cooperation.

Responsibility entails being accountable for one's actions and their consequences. A responsible person does not blame others for their faults and takes ownership of their decisions. This value is closely linked to integrity because it reinforces the idea that one should stand by their actions and beliefs, even in adverse circumstances.

Fairness is about acting justly and equitably. It involves making impartial decisions and recognizing each individual's needs and circumstances. Fair people ensure that their own biases or personal interests do not cloud their judgments. This is particularly important in positions of power, where the temptation to favor certain interests over others can be strong.

Compassion involves empathy and caring for others. It moves beyond mere tolerance of others to actively seeking to understand and alleviate their difficulties. Compassionate individuals are often admired for their ability to maintain their moral principles and act kindly towards others, even in challenging situations.

Living with integrity means that these values are not just abstract concepts but are evident in our daily actions. It means making choices that are not only good for oneself but also considerate of others and the greater good. For instance, a person of integrity will not cheat on a test, knowing that it undermines their own learning and the trust others place in them. Similarly, at work, such an individual will not take credit for someone else's work or use their position to exploit others.

One of the challenges of living with integrity in the modern world is the constant pressure to compromise on these values. Whether it's the allure of quick gains through dishonest means or the ease with which one can hide behind anonymity, especially online, there are numerous temptations that test our resolve to live ethically.

Moreover, the complexity of modern ethical dilemmas can sometimes make it difficult to know the right course of action. Issues such as environmental responsibility, digital privacy, and global economic inequality require us to consider a broad range of factors and often to balance conflicting values. Here, integrity involves a commitment to continual learning and self-reflection, enabling us to make informed, ethical decisions.

Self-reflection is particularly vital. It involves regularly examining one's values and actions and assessing whether they align with one's ethical beliefs. This can be challenging, as it may lead to recognizing faults in oneself that are uncomfortable to admit. However, such honesty with oneself is a crucial step in living with integrity.

Finally, integrity is not just a personal virtue but a societal one. When leaders display integrity, they inspire it in others. Communities where integrity is valued and demonstrated tend to be stronger, more cooperative, and more peaceful. In such societies, individuals feel a greater sense of belonging and purpose, knowing that their actions contribute to the common good.

These values provide the framework through which we can navigate the complexities of life, making decisions that reflect not only our interests but also our deepest beliefs about what is right and good. Living with integrity thus enriches our lives, provides us with a sense of self-respect, and contributes to a better world. In a time filled with challenges and opportunities alike, integrity is more important than ever, guiding us toward ethical enlightenment and a life lived with true purpose.

"Integrity is not just about doing the right thing when no one is watching; it's about aligning our actions with our deepest values, even when faced with the toughest decisions."

CHAPTER TWO

Empathy in Action: Cultivating Compassion in Everyday Life

Empathy is the ability to understand and share the feelings of another person. It is a fundamental part of being human, enabling us to connect with others on a deep emotional level.

Empathy involves more than just feeling sorry for someone who is suffering. It is about genuinely understanding what another person is going through, imagining yourself in their place, and feeling what they might be feeling. By doing so, we are better equipped to respond in ways that are truly helpful and supportive. Empathy nurtures compassion, which drives us to take action to alleviate the suffering of others.

The cultivation of empathy begins with active listening. This means paying close attention to what someone is saying without immediately formulating a response or judgment. When we listen actively, we give the other person space to express themselves fully. We observe their body language, listen to the tone of their voice, and pay attention to the emotions behind their words. This level of attentiveness shows that we care and are genuinely interested in understanding their experience.

Beyond listening, empathy requires an open mind. Often, our own experiences and biases can cloud our ability to see things from another person's perspective. To cultivate empathy, we must challenge our preconceptions and make a conscious effort to understand others' viewpoints, even if they differ significantly from our own. This does not mean we have to agree with everything they say, but rather that we strive to understand where they are coming from.

Empathy also involves emotional resonance, where we allow ourselves to feel what another person might be feeling. This can be challenging, particularly in situations where the emotions involved are intense or painful. However, feeling with someone, rather than just feeling for them, can deepen our connection and make our support more meaningful.

One of the most powerful ways to put empathy into action is through acts of kindness. These don't have to be grand gestures; small, everyday actions can have a profound impact. For instance, offering a sincere compliment, helping a colleague with a difficult task, or simply making time to check in with a friend can all be expressions of empathy. These acts of kindness show that we recognize others' needs and are willing to help meet them.

Empathy can also extend beyond our immediate circles to the broader community. Volunteering at local shelters, participating in community clean-up days, or supporting local charities are all ways to demonstrate empathy on a larger scale. These activities not only help those in need but also strengthen our communal bonds and remind us of the interconnectedness of our lives.

However, while empathy is a powerful tool for fostering compassion, it is also important to manage its emotional demands. Empathizing deeply with many people, especially those experiencing significant distress, can lead to emotional burnout. This is where self-care becomes crucial. Ensuring that we take time to replenish our emotional reserves and seek support when needed helps us maintain our capacity for empathy without becoming overwhelmed.

Moreover, empathy must be genuine to be effective. It cannot be forced or faked; people can usually tell when our interest or concern is not sincere. Developing true empathy may require us to confront and work through our own emotional barriers. This process, while sometimes difficult, can lead to significant personal growth and deeper relationships.

Ultimately, empathy enriches our lives. It enhances our relationships, making them more meaningful and supportive. It encourages a kinder, more compassionate society by reminding us of our shared human experiences and vulnerabilities. In a world that often seems divided and indifferent, empathy can be a bridge that connects us, fostering understanding and cooperation across diverse communities.

Cultivating empathy in everyday life involves active listening, keeping an open mind, resonating emotionally, performing acts of kindness, managing its emotional demands, and ensuring authenticity. By embedding these practices into our daily routines, we can bring compassion into action, making a tangible difference in our lives and the lives of those around us. Empathy is not just a personal quality but a collective asset that can transform our communities, making them more connected and caring. As we navigate the complexities of modern life, the practice of empathy stands as a beacon of hope, guiding us toward a more compassionate and harmonious existence.

"Compassion is the bridge that connects hearts, allowing us to see ourselves in others and to extend kindness without boundaries."

Decisions at the Crossroads: Navigating Personal Ethical Dilemmas

Ethical dilemmas are situations where we are forced to choose between two or more conflicting moral principles. These dilemmas challenge us, pushing us to reflect deeply on our values and the potential outcomes of our decisions.

Personal ethical dilemmas are common in our everyday lives. They can range from deciding whether to return a lost wallet, to choosing between telling the truth or protecting a friend's feelings. Each dilemma presents a unique challenge, often with no clear-cut solution. However, the process of confronting these dilemmas can help us refine our moral compass and strengthen our character.

The first step in navigating ethical dilemmas is to clearly identify the conflicting values involved. For instance, if you find a lost wallet, the conflict might be between the desire to keep the money (self-interest) and the duty to return it to its owner (honesty and responsibility). Recognizing the specific values in conflict allows you to weigh them more carefully against each other.

Once the values are identified, it is helpful to consider the potential consequences of each choice. Who will be affected by your decision? What are the short-term and long-term impacts? Thinking through the consequences can help you better understand the stakes involved and guide you toward a decision that minimizes harm while maximizing benefits.

Reflecting on similar past experiences can also provide valuable insights. Consider times when you faced similar choices and think about the decisions you made. What were the outcomes? How did you feel about your choice afterward? Learning from past experiences can inform your current decision-making process, helping you to make more thoughtful and consistent choices.

Another crucial aspect of navigating ethical dilemmas is seeking advice from trusted individuals. Friends, family members, mentors, or colleagues can offer different perspectives that might not have occurred to you. They can challenge your assumptions, raise new questions, or reinforce your initial inclinations. However, it's important to choose advisors who are themselves ethical and who understand the importance of moral values.

Sometimes, ethical dilemmas can be resolved by finding creative alternatives that satisfy all conflicting values to some extent. For instance, if you're faced with a choice between telling a hurtful truth and lying, you might find a way to express the truth more gently, or to focus on the most constructive parts of the message. This approach requires flexibility and a willingness to think outside the traditional choices presented.

When making the final decision, it is essential to act with integrity. This means being true to your deepest values and making a choice that you can stand by, even in the face of adversity. Integrity does not guarantee that the choice will be easy or that it will please everyone involved, but it ensures that the decision aligns with your moral principles.

After making a decision, it is beneficial to reflect on the process and the outcome. What did you learn from the experience? How did it affect your understanding of your values? Reflection not only helps in personal growth but also prepares you for future dilemmas by reinforcing your ethical decision-making skills.

It's important to remember that navigating ethical dilemmas is not about achieving perfection. We are all human and sometimes make mistakes. What matters is that we strive to act ethically, learn from our experiences, and continue to refine our ability to make moral choices.

Navigating personal ethical dilemmas involves identifying conflicting values, considering the consequences of each option, drawing on past experiences, seeking advice, finding creative solutions, acting with integrity, and reflecting on the decisions made. These steps provide a structured approach to making tough choices, helping us to act in ways that are consistent with our values and beneficial to those around us. By thoughtfully addressing ethical dilemmas, we cultivate a deeper understanding of ourselves and contribute to a more ethical and just society.

*"In the crossroads of life, our ethical compass
guides us towards the path of righteousness,
urging us to choose what is right over what is easy.*

CHAPTER FOUR

The Ethics of Relationships: Honesty and Trust in Personal Connections

The fabric of all relationships, whether they are personal, professional, or casual, is woven with the threads of honesty and trust. These elements are not just desirable but essential for the health and longevity of any connection.

Honesty in relationships goes beyond merely not lying. It encompasses being truthful, transparent, and sincere in all interactions. Being honest means sharing your feelings, thoughts, and intentions openly and respectfully. It requires courage and vulnerability, especially when the truth might be painful or unwelcome. However, the importance of honesty extends beyond individual interactions; it builds a foundation of trust, which is crucial for any relationship to thrive.

Trust is the confidence you place in another person to act with integrity, reliability, and care. It is built over time, through consistent and dependable actions. Trust makes it possible for relationships to grow, as it allows people to feel safe and secure.

Without trust, relationships often become superficial or unstable, as there is always uncertainty about the other person's motives or actions.

The challenge in maintaining honesty and trust in relationships often comes from ethical dilemmas where interests or desires conflict. For example, you may find yourself in a situation where telling the truth could hurt someone you care about. Or, you might be tempted to hide the truth to avoid conflict or punishment. These situations test the strength of your ethical principles and require careful consideration and sensitivity.

Navigating these dilemmas starts with a clear understanding of the values that underpin your relationships. What is more important in the long run—avoiding short-term pain or maintaining the integrity of the relationship? Often, opting for honesty, even when it is difficult, proves to be the better choice for long-term trust and relationship health.

It's also important to consider how honesty is conveyed. Communication should be done with kindness and tact. The way a message is delivered can significantly affect how it is received. Expressing truth should not be an excuse for being hurtful. Instead, being honest should be about fostering understanding and growth within the relationship.

Another aspect of maintaining ethical relationships is dealing with breaches of trust. If trust is broken, it can be challenging to rebuild. The process often involves sincere apologies, a commitment to change behavior, and, crucially, time. Both parties must want to repair the relationship and be willing to work through the discomfort that might entail.

Sometimes, ethical relationship dilemmas are not about truth versus lies but about respecting boundaries and privacy. Not all truths need to be shared if sharing them violates someone's privacy or autonomy. Balancing transparency and discretion is another skill that requires ethical judgment and understanding.

The ethics of relationships also extends to how we handle disagreements or conflicts. Resolving conflicts ethically involves dealing with issues directly and respectfully, rather than resorting to manipulation or passive-aggressiveness. It means striving for solutions that acknowledge and address everyone's needs, not just winning an argument.

In practice, maintaining honesty and trust in relationships means being consistently reliable, not just when it is convenient. It means showing up, keeping promises, and proving through actions that you are trustworthy. It also means being honest with yourself about your feelings and motives in a relationship.

Reflecting on the health of your relationships can often provide insights into how well you are practicing these ethical principles. Are your relationships marked by mutual respect and understanding? Do you feel safe and valued? Answering these questions honestly can help you identify areas where you may need to improve your approach to relationship ethics.

The ethics of relationships revolves around honesty and trust. These principles are crucial for building and maintaining strong, healthy relationships. By prioritizing transparency, reliability, and respect, and navigating ethical dilemmas with care and consideration, we can foster deeper connections with those around us. Relationships built on such a foundation are more likely to withstand the tests of time and conflict, providing lasting support and mutual growth.

"*Honesty and trust are the foundation stones of every meaningful relationship, cementing bonds that withstand the tests of time and adversity.*"

CHAPTER FIVE

Global Citizenship: The Ethics of Living in a Connected World

In today's interconnected world, the concept of global citizenship is becoming increasingly important. Being a global citizen means recognizing that we are part of a worldwide community and that our actions have implications not only for ourselves but for others across the globe.

Global citizenship involves a sense of shared identity beyond national borders. It is about understanding the interconnectedness of all people, regardless of where they live. This perspective encourages us to think about the social, environmental, and economic impacts of our actions on a global scale. It compels us to act in ways that promote the well-being of all people, not just those within our immediate community or country.

One of the foundational ethical principles of global citizenship is empathy, which we discussed earlier. Empathy on a global scale involves an awareness of the lives of people in different parts of the world and an appreciation of their circumstances. It means caring about the rights and welfare of people in distant countries as much as we care about those closer to home. This global empathy helps drive actions that are considerate of the broader human community.

Another crucial aspect of global citizenship is sustainability. Our planet faces numerous environmental challenges, such as climate change, deforestation, and water scarcity. These issues require a global response. Ethical global citizens recognize the importance of sustainable practices that preserve the Earth for future generations. This involves making choices that reduce environmental impact, such as minimizing waste, using energy efficiently, and supporting policies and businesses that are environmentally responsible.

Global economic justice is another important dimension of global citizenship. The world is marked by significant economic inequalities, with stark disparities in wealth and access to resources. As global citizens, we face the ethical challenge of how to address these inequalities. This might involve supporting fair trade, advocating for policies that aid economic development in poorer countries, or working to ensure that workers everywhere are treated fairly and can earn a living wage.

Cultural respect and tolerance also play a significant role in the ethics of global citizenship. In a connected world, we encounter a diverse range of cultures and lifestyles. Respecting cultural differences and seeking to understand rather than judge or change people is crucial. This respect fosters a more peaceful and cooperative international community.

One of the biggest challenges in living as a global citizen is overcoming the "out of sight, out of mind" mentality. It's easy to ignore issues that don't directly affect us or that occur far away. However, ethical global citizenship requires us to be informed and proactive about global issues. This can include educating ourselves and others about world events, supporting international aid efforts, and advocating for policies that benefit the global community.

Ethical dilemmas often arise when the interests of global citizenship conflict with personal or national interests. For example, buying cheaper products made in poor working conditions abroad may benefit consumers financially but harm workers globally. Navigating such dilemmas requires careful consideration of the ethical implications of our choices and a commitment to actions that align with the principles of global citizenship.

Participating in the global community also means advocating for global governance that upholds human rights and promotes peace. Supporting international organizations and agreements that aim to address global challenges is part of ethical global citizenship. By doing so, we contribute to efforts that ensure fairness, security, and cooperation among nations.

The ethics of global citizenship are centered around empathy, sustainability, economic justice, cultural respect, and active participation in the global community. These principles guide us in making decisions that are not only good for us individually but are also beneficial for the global community. As we navigate our interconnected world, embracing our role as global citizens can lead to a more ethical, just, and sustainable future for everyone. Living with this global perspective enriches our lives and helps us make a positive impact on the world.

"As citizens of a global community, our actions ripple across borders, reminding us of our collective responsibility to nurture and protect our shared home, Earth."

CHAPTER SIX

Ethical Consumption: Making Responsible Choices as a Consumer

In today's global economy, the choices we make as consumers have far-reaching impacts on the environment, economies, and societies around the world. Ethical consumption involves making purchasing decisions that are not only good for us but also beneficial, or at least not harmful, to others.

Ethical consumption starts with awareness. It requires us to be informed about where our products come from, how they are made, and the impact their production has on the environment and society. This awareness helps us recognize the real cost of the goods we purchase—not just in terms of money, but also in terms of the social and environmental toll. For example, cheap clothing might seem like a bargain, but if it's produced in factories where workers are treated poorly, the true cost is much higher.

One of the key aspects of ethical consumption is considering the sustainability of products. This means choosing goods that are produced in ways that do not deplete natural resources or cause significant harm to the environment. Sustainable products might include those made from recycled materials, items that are energy-efficient, or goods produced using practices that minimize environmental degradation. By prioritizing sustainability in our purchasing decisions, we contribute to the health of the planet and support industries that are working towards ecological responsibility.

Fair trade is another important element of ethical consumption. Fair trade products are those that ensure fair wages and working conditions for workers, particularly in developing countries. When we choose fair trade, we help combat exploitation in the global supply chain and support communities in maintaining a decent standard of living. Fair trade also promotes better environmental practices and aims to empower farmers and workers to invest in their communities.

Ethical consumption also involves reducing waste. This means thinking about the life cycle of the products we buy—how long we will use them, and what will happen to them when we no longer need them. Opting for products with less packaging, choosing items that are durable and repairable, and recycling or donating goods instead of throwing them away are all practices that reduce waste and lessen our environmental impact.

However, ethical consumption is not just about buying the right things; it's also about buying less in general. Consumer culture often encourages us to buy more than we need, leading to wasteful production and consumption patterns. By consciously choosing to buy fewer items and focusing on quality and necessity, we can reduce our ecological footprint and promote a more sustainable form of consumption.

Making ethical choices as a consumer can sometimes be challenging, especially when information about product origins and manufacturing processes is not readily available. It can also be more expensive to purchase sustainable or fair trade products. However, the long-term benefits of these choices—for the planet, for global workers, and for our own well-being—make them worthwhile.

To practice ethical consumption, start by educating yourself about the products you buy. Look for certifications like organic, fair trade, and energy-efficient labels that help identify products that meet higher ethical standards. Support businesses and brands that are transparent about their supply chains and committed to ethical practices. And remember, every purchase is a vote for the kind of world you want to live in.

Ethical consumption is about making informed and conscientious choices as a consumer. It involves considering the environmental and social impacts of our purchases and opting for products that align with our ethical standards. By embracing ethical consumption, we take responsibility for our part in the global economy and contribute to a more just and sustainable world. It is an ongoing commitment that requires us to be proactive, informed, and sometimes willing to make sacrifices for the greater good. Through our daily choices, we can make a significant impact and drive change toward a better future.

"*Every purchase we make is a vote for the kind of world we want to live in, reminding us of the power of ethical consumption to drive positive change.*"

CHAPTER SEVEN

Sustainability and Ethics: Protecting Our Planet for Future Generations

Sustainability is a concept that has become increasingly critical as the world faces environmental crises such as climate change, biodiversity loss, and pollution. At its core, sustainability is about meeting our current needs without compromising the ability of future generations to meet their own. Here, I will explore the ethical dimensions of sustainability and how we can actively contribute to the preservation and enhancement of our planet's resources for those who will come after us.

The ethical imperative for sustainability stems from a recognition of our responsibility not only to our own generation but also to future ones. This sense of duty requires us to reconsider our relationship with the natural world and our consumption habits. Ethically, it challenges us to reflect on the impacts of our actions and to make choices that contribute positively to the environment.

One of the first steps in adopting a sustainable lifestyle is understanding the impact of human activities on the environment. This includes acknowledging how our use of resources like water, energy, and raw materials contributes to environmental degradation. For example, the energy we consume in our homes and the fuel we use in our vehicles have direct effects on air quality and climate change. Similarly, the waste we produce can harm ecosystems if not properly managed.

To address these impacts, ethical sustainability involves reducing our ecological footprint. This can be achieved through various means, such as conserving energy, using water efficiently, reducing waste, and choosing sustainable products. For instance, turning off lights when not in use, fixing leaks, recycling, and opting for products with minimal packaging are all practical ways to live more sustainably.

Another key aspect of ethical sustainability is the support of renewable energy sources. Transitioning from fossil fuels to renewable energy sources like solar, wind, and hydroelectric power can significantly reduce our carbon footprint. This shift not only helps mitigate climate change but also reduces air and water pollution, contributing to a healthier environment.

Ethical sustainability also encompasses the preservation of biodiversity. Biodiversity, the variety of life on Earth, is crucial for ecosystem stability, agricultural diversity, and the overall health of the planet. Protecting habitats, supporting conservation efforts, and being mindful of our interaction with wildlife are all ethical actions that contribute to maintaining biodiversity.

Beyond individual actions, ethical sustainability requires collective efforts. This involves advocating for policies that protect the environment and support sustainable practices. It means supporting organizations and businesses that prioritize sustainability in their operations and products. On a larger scale, it involves international cooperation to tackle global environmental issues, such as climate change and ocean pollution.

Ethical dilemmas often arise in the context of sustainability. For instance, economic development and environmental protection can sometimes seem at odds. Balancing these needs requires thoughtful decision-making that considers both the short-term benefits to current populations and the long-term consequences for future generations. It involves finding innovative solutions that drive economic growth while preserving the environment.

Furthermore, the ethical approach to sustainability includes ensuring that environmental benefits and burdens are shared fairly. This means addressing environmental justice issues, such as ensuring that no community bears a disproportionate share of negative environmental impacts. It also involves ensuring that all communities have equal access to natural resources and the benefits derived from sustainable practices.

Sustainability and ethics are deeply intertwined. Protecting our planet for future generations is not just an environmental issue but a moral imperative. By adopting sustainable practices and making ethical choices, we can help ensure that future generations inherit a world that is not only livable but flourishing. Our actions today are crucial in shaping the future of our planet, and each step we take towards sustainability is a step towards a more ethical and equitable world. Through awareness, personal action, advocacy, and collaboration, we can make a significant impact on the health and well-being of our planet and its inhabitants.

"Sustainability is not just a buzzword; it's a commitment to preserving the delicate balance of life on Earth for generations to come."

The Power of Community: Building Supportive Ethical Networks

Community plays a fundamental role in shaping our values, actions, and interactions. In a world that often seems driven by individual achievement and competition, the strength of community bonds can be a powerful force for fostering ethical behavior and mutual support. We should surely know the importance of building supportive ethical networks and how these communities can enhance our lives and the world around us.

The concept of community has evolved significantly over time, especially with the advent of digital technology. Today, communities are not only formed by geographical proximity but also by shared interests, goals, and values that span across the globe. These networks provide a sense of belonging and support, offering a platform for individuals to connect, share, and grow together.

Building a supportive ethical network starts with the recognition of our interdependence. No one exists in isolation; our actions affect others, just as their actions affect us. This mutual influence forms the ethical basis of community—it underscores the responsibility we have towards each other. Communities thrive when their members commit to honesty, respect, empathy, and cooperation, ensuring that everyone's needs and well-being are considered.

One of the key benefits of being part of an ethical community is the support system it offers. Life can present challenging situations where moral guidance and emotional support are crucial. In these times, a community can provide the advice, encouragement, and help needed to navigate difficult decisions and situations. This support is not just about overcoming challenges but also about celebrating successes and milestones together, which strengthens the bonds within the community.

Ethical networks also play a crucial role in personal and collective growth. Through regular interaction and engagement, community members can learn from each other, gaining new perspectives and insights that enrich their understanding and behaviors. This learning is particularly valuable when it comes to ethics, as discussing real-life scenarios and theoretical dilemmas with others can deepen one's ethical reasoning and decision-making skills.

Moreover, communities have the power to mobilize resources and efforts towards common goals, such as local charity drives, community clean-ups, or larger advocacy campaigns. The collective action of a community can achieve much more than individuals acting alone. This is evident in movements that have led to significant social change—often, these movements begin as small communities of dedicated individuals who share a commitment to a cause.

Building and maintaining ethical networks requires effort and intentionality. It involves creating environments where open communication, trust, and respect are prioritized. This means setting up clear norms and values that guide interactions and making sure that all members feel valued and heard. It also involves dealing with conflicts in a constructive manner that respects differing viewpoints and seeks mutually beneficial resolutions.

However, ethical communities are not just about harmony and agreement. They should also be spaces for challenging each other and fostering resilience. This means encouraging members to question, debate, and refine their ideas and behaviors in a supportive setting. Such dynamics ensure that the community does not become an echo chamber but a vibrant, evolving space that adapits to new challenges and opportunities.

Inclusivity is another important aspect of building supportive networks. A truly ethical community seeks to include diverse perspectives and experiences, which enrich the community's understanding and effectiveness. Inclusivity means actively reaching out to and involving people from different backgrounds, ages, and walks of life. It also involves making sure that everyone has an opportunity to contribute and participate meaningfully.

The power of community in building supportive ethical networks is immense. These networks enhance our lives by providing support, fostering personal and collective growth, and enabling us to achieve greater impacts through collective action. By investing in our communities and prioritizing ethical principles in our interactions, we not only enrich our own lives but also contribute to a more just and compassionate world. Building and nurturing these networks is an ongoing journey—one that requires patience, commitment, and a deep appreciation for the value of connection and ethical solidarity.

"In the tapestry of community, each thread represents a unique individual, but it is only when woven together that we create a fabric strong enough to weather life's storms."

CHAPTER NINE

Workplace Integrity: Ethics in Professional Environments

Integrity in the workplace is crucial for fostering a culture of trust, respect, and efficiency. Professional environments thrive when they are grounded in ethical principles that guide the behavior of all members, from the highest levels of leadership to entry-level positions. Through this chapter I wish to share the concept of workplace integrity and how it can be cultivated to create a more ethical and productive professional environment.

Workplace integrity involves a commitment to ethical principles in all aspects of work, from how decisions are made to how individuals interact with each other. It encompasses several key components, including honesty, fairness, respect, and responsibility. These elements are not just abstract ideals but practical necessities that affect the daily operations and the overall success of an organization.

Honesty in the workplace means being truthful in communications and actions. It involves providing accurate information, admitting mistakes, and avoiding deceitful behavior. Honesty builds trust among team members and stakeholders, and it ensures that decisions are made based on accurate and transparent information. For example, when a manager reports on the progress of a project, being honest about the challenges faced not only helps to address these issues effectively but also builds trust and credibility.

Fairness is another critical component of workplace integrity. It involves treating all employees and colleagues equitably and without discrimination. Fairness in the workplace is reflected in how opportunities for advancement are given, how resources are allocated, and how disciplinary actions are handled. It ensures that everyone feels valued and treated justly, which can enhance morale and productivity.

Respect in a professional setting means acknowledging the dignity of each person in the workplace. It involves listening to others' viewpoints, valuing their contributions, and interacting in a polite and considerate manner. Respect also extends to respecting people's time and boundaries, such as by not expecting employees to consistently work long hours without recognition or compensation.

Responsibility in the workplace encompasses taking ownership of one's roles and actions. It involves fulfilling duties diligently, being accountable for one's contributions, and taking initiative to solve problems. When employees embody responsibility, they not only enhance their own performance but also contribute positively to the organization's goals.

Cultivating workplace integrity starts with leadership. Leaders set the tone for ethical behavior in the organization. When leaders demonstrate integrity through their actions—such as making fair decisions, communicating honestly, and treating others with respect—they model the behavior expected of everyone in the organization. Leadership commitment to ethics can be further reinforced through policies and practices that promote integrity, such as codes of conduct, ethical training programs, and systems for anonymously reporting unethical behavior.

Another important aspect of promoting integrity in the workplace is creating an environment where ethical behavior is rewarded and unethical behavior is addressed. Recognizing and rewarding employees who demonstrate ethical behavior encourages others to follow suit. Conversely, consistently addressing unethical behavior through appropriate disciplinary actions sends a clear message about the organization's commitment to integrity.

Moreover, fostering open communication is vital in maintaining workplace integrity. Employees should feel comfortable voicing concerns, asking questions, and expressing dissenting opinions without fear of retaliation. An environment that encourages open communication allows for the free exchange of ideas, promotes transparency, and helps identify and resolve ethical issues more effectively.

Challenges to workplace integrity often arise from conflicting interests, such as the pressure to meet business objectives that might tempt individuals to act unethically. Navigating these challenges requires a clear ethical framework and a commitment to maintaining integrity even when faced with difficult choices. For instance, a sales team under pressure to meet quotas might be tempted to mislead customers about a product's capabilities. In such situations, adherence to ethical standards is crucial, not only to maintain trust with customers but also to uphold the company's reputation.

Workplace integrity is foundational to the success and sustainability of any organization. It enhances trust, improves teamwork, and drives better business results. By committing to ethical principles and fostering a culture that supports honesty, fairness, respect, and responsibility, organizations can create a positive and productive work environment. As we navigate the complexities of the modern professional landscape, the role of integrity remains more critical than ever, underpinning ethical conduct and guiding organizations towards a prosperous and principled future.

"Ethical leadership is not about wielding power;
it's about inspiring others to reach their full
potential and fostering a culture of integrity and
excellence."

CHAPTER TEN

Digital Dilemmas: Ethics in the Age of Technology

In the digital age, technology permeates almost every aspect of our lives, from how we communicate and work to how we shop and entertain ourselves. While technology offers incredible benefits, it also introduces complex ethical dilemmas that require careful consideration and responsible handling.

One of the primary ethical dilemmas in the digital age is privacy. With the vast amount of personal information collected by websites, social media platforms, and other online services, maintaining privacy has become increasingly challenging. Companies often track user activity to gather data for advertising and other purposes, sometimes without the user's explicit consent. The ethical question arises: how much privacy are individuals entitled to, and what responsibilities do companies have to protect that privacy?

Respecting user privacy means implementing strong data protection measures, being transparent about what data is collected and how it is used, and providing users with control over their information. For individuals, ethical behavior involves being aware of the privacy settings on the platforms they use and making informed choices about what information to share online.

Another significant ethical issue in the digital realm is misinformation. The spread of false or misleading information can have serious consequences, from influencing elections to endangering public health. The ethical challenge here is to balance freedom of expression with the need to prevent harm caused by misinformation. Social media companies, news outlets, and individual users all have roles to play in addressing this issue. Companies need to develop and enforce policies that minimize the spread of false information while promoting transparency and accountability. Users, on the other hand, should practice critical thinking and verify information before sharing it.

The rise of artificial intelligence (AI) introduces further ethical considerations. AI systems are used in a variety of applications, from autonomous vehicles and healthcare diagnostics to personal assistants and recommendation systems. While AI can improve efficiency and solve complex problems, it also raises issues such as bias, accountability, and the displacement of jobs. Ethical AI use involves ensuring that these systems are designed and deployed in a way that is fair, transparent, and respects human rights. Developers and companies must consider the potential impacts of AI and strive to mitigate negative outcomes, such as discrimination or privacy breaches.

Cybersecurity is another critical area of digital ethics. As our reliance on technology grows, so does the risk of cyber attacks that can lead to data breaches, financial loss, and other damages. Ethical behavior in cybersecurity involves not only implementing robust security measures but also promoting a culture of security awareness among users and employees. Organizations have a responsibility to protect their systems and data from cyber threats, while individuals must be vigilant about their own digital security practices.

In addition to these challenges, the digital age also brings ethical questions related to intellectual property. With the ease of copying and sharing digital content, copyright infringement has become a widespread issue. Ethically navigating this area means respecting the rights of creators by not distributing or consuming pirated content and supporting fair use policies.

Navigating the ethical dilemmas of the digital age requires a combination of personal responsibility, corporate accountability, and regulatory oversight. Individuals must be educated about the implications of their digital actions and make ethical choices in their use of technology. Companies must prioritize ethical considerations in the design and implementation of their technologies and be transparent with users about their practices. Governments and regulatory bodies must develop and enforce laws that protect individuals and promote fair practices.

The digital age presents a range of ethical dilemmas that reflect the complex interplay between technology and society. By understanding these challenges and committing to ethical behavior, we can harness the benefits of technology while minimizing its risks. Whether as users, developers, or regulators, we all have a part to play in ensuring that technology is used in ways that respect privacy, promote truth, and foster an equitable and secure digital world. Through thoughtful consideration and ethical action, we can navigate the digital dilemmas of our time and move towards a more responsible and ethical technological future.

"Conflict is inevitable, but it is in the resolution of disagreements that we truly demonstrate our commitment to fairness, empathy, and understanding."

CHAPTER ELEVEN

Ethical Leadership: Inspiring Integrity in Others

Ethical leadership is a crucial element in fostering environments of integrity, respect, and constructive collaboration, whether in organizations, communities, or nations.

An ethical leader is someone who leads by example and guides others not merely through words but through consistent, moral action. These leaders possess qualities such as honesty, fairness, compassion, and courage. They strive to make decisions that benefit not just themselves or their organizations, but also the broader community and future generations. This approach to leadership does not just create a more ethical environment; it also builds trust, enhances reputation, and improves long-term outcomes for their organizations and communities.

The foundation of ethical leadership lies in self-awareness. Ethical leaders are conscious of their values and beliefs and understand how these principles influence their decisions and actions. They reflect regularly on their behavior and are open to feedback about their ethical conduct. This self-awareness helps them maintain a high standard of integrity and guides them in inspiring the same in others.

Communication is another key aspect of ethical leadership. Ethical leaders communicate openly and honestly. They are clear about their expectations and the ethical standards they uphold. Through transparent communication, they create a culture of trust where team members feel valued and informed. Furthermore, these leaders use communication to foster a sense of shared responsibility among their team members, encouraging them to take ownership of their actions and their consequences.

Ethical leaders also demonstrate empathy and fairness in dealing with others. They strive to understand the perspectives and needs of their team members and other stakeholders. This empathy allows them to make more informed and considerate decisions. Fairness is evident in how they distribute resources, reward performance, and provide opportunities for growth and development. By treating everyone with equity and respect, ethical leaders ensure that no one feels marginalized or undervalued.

Moreover, ethical leaders are committed to serving others. They prioritize the well-being of their team members and the community over personal gain. This service-oriented mindset often leads to more collaborative and supportive work environments, where the focus is on collective success rather than individual achievement. Such environments encourage team members to also act ethically and support one another.

Accountability is another critical element of ethical leadership. Ethical leaders hold themselves and others accountable for their actions. They do not shy away from taking responsibility when things go wrong, nor do they tolerate unethical behavior in others. By setting this standard, they ensure that ethical practices are followed consistently, reinforcing a culture of integrity.

Challenging situations often test ethical leaders the most. In such times, these leaders remain committed to their principles, even when faced with difficult choices. For instance, an ethical leader facing financial difficulties in a company might refuse to cut corners or engage in fraudulent activities to save costs. Instead, they look for solutions that uphold their ethical standards, such as transparently restructuring or seeking honest feedback from stakeholders.

Ethical leaders also inspire integrity by creating and nurturing an ethical framework within their organization. This includes establishing clear ethical policies, providing training on ethical issues, and implementing systems that support ethical decision-making. By institutionalizing ethics, leaders make it an integral part of the organizational culture.

Ethical leadership is about more than just making the right choices. It's about inspiring and enabling others to do the same. Ethical leaders influence their organizations and communities profoundly, shaping them into places where integrity, respect, and fairness are not just encouraged but expected. By embodying these values, leaders not only achieve greater personal and organizational success but also contribute to a more just and ethical world. Through their actions, ethical leaders inspire current and future generations to carry forward the mantle of integrity.

"Amidst the cacophony of voices in the media, it is our ethical duty to seek truth, discern fact from fiction, and uphold the principles of honesty and integrity."

CHAPTER TWELVE

Conflict and Resolution: Ethical Approaches to Disagreements

Conflict is a natural part of human relationships, arising from differences in opinions, desires, or values. While often viewed negatively, conflict can be a force for positive change and personal growth when approached ethically. Let me share how to handle disagreements with integrity, promoting understanding and respect even in the face of conflict.

Ethical resolution of conflicts hinges on the principles of fairness, respect, honesty, and empathy. These principles provide a framework that guides our actions and decisions during disagreements, ensuring that all parties are treated justly and with dignity.

The first step in ethically approaching a conflict is to genuinely understand the perspectives involved. This requires active listening, a skill that involves more than just hearing words; it requires interpreting the underlying feelings and thoughts behind them. By listening actively, we show respect for the speaker, validate their feelings, and gain a deeper understanding of the conflict's root causes. It also helps to de-escalate tension as it shows we are committed to understanding rather than just winning the argument.

Honesty is also crucial in resolving conflicts. This involves expressing one's own views clearly and directly while remaining respectful. It means being truthful about one's feelings and the impact of the situation while avoiding exaggeration or manipulation of facts to sway the outcome unfairly. Honest communication opens the door for genuine resolution and trust-building.

Empathy plays a vital role in ethical conflict resolution. By striving to understand and feel what the other person is experiencing, we can better navigate the disagreement. Empathy helps in recognizing the emotions involved and addressing them sensitively, which can transform the nature of the conflict, often leading to more compassionate and fitting resolutions.

Another key element is fairness. In conflicts, ethical behavior demands that we seek fair outcomes that consider the well-being of all involved. This might mean compromising or finding a middle ground where all parties feel their views and needs have been considered. Fairness also involves acknowledging any biases we might bring to the situation and actively working to minimize their impact on the resolution process.

Once these principles are in place, there are several strategies that can be employed to move towards resolution. One effective approach is mediation, where a neutral third party helps facilitate the discussion and guide both sides towards a mutually acceptable solution. Mediation can be particularly helpful when emotions run high, as the mediator can ensure that the dialogue remains respectful and constructive.

Negotiation is another strategy where the parties involved discuss their needs and interests to find a solution that benefits both sides. Effective negotiation requires clear communication, willingness to compromise, and a thorough understanding of each party's priorities. This process not only resolves the immediate conflict but can also strengthen relationships by building trust and understanding.

In cases where conflicts are complex or deeply entrenched, it may be beneficial to adopt a problem-solving approach. This method involves identifying the underlying issues, generating a range of potential solutions, and then evaluating these solutions based on how well they meet the needs of all parties. This approach can lead to innovative and lasting resolutions that might not have been considered in a more confrontational or adversarial setting.

An ethical approach to conflict and resolution also means being prepared to accept that not all conflicts can be completely resolved to everyone's satisfaction. In such cases, agreeing to disagree may be the most ethical outcome. It allows for the preservation of relationships and respect, even when consensus is unattainable.

Ethical approaches to conflict resolution are about more than just settling disputes; they are about doing so in a way that upholds the dignity and respect of all involved. By prioritizing fairness, respect, honesty, and empathy, and employing strategies such as mediation, negotiation, and problem-solving, we can transform conflicts into opportunities for growth and understanding. These approaches not only resolve the immediate issues but also contribute to a culture of ethical behavior and mutual respect, which is essential for any community or organization to thrive.

"Financial ethics demand more than just fiscal
responsibility; they require us to use our resources
wisely and ethically, for the betterment of society
as a whole.

CHAPTER THIRTEEN

The Ethics of Information: Navigating Truth in the Media

In today's information age, media plays a pivotal role in shaping our perceptions of the world. However, the vast amount of information available and the varied sources from which it comes can sometimes make it challenging to discern truth from falsehood.

The ethical handling of information by media outlets is critical because it impacts public opinion, democracy, and the very fabric of society. Ethical journalism is rooted in truthfulness, fairness, impartiality, and accountability. However, with the rise of digital media, the speed at which news is reported can sometimes prioritize timeliness over accuracy, leading to misinformation or incomplete stories. Moreover, the economic pressures to attract viewers or readers can result in sensationalism, where news is presented in a way that is intended to provoke public interest or excitement at the expense of accuracy.

For consumers of media, navigating this landscape requires a critical eye and an ethical approach to processing information. The first step in this process is to recognize the potential for bias in all forms of media. Every news outlet has its perspectives which can influence how stories are reported. Understanding this helps us to critically evaluate the information presented and seek out multiple sources to get a more balanced view of the events.

Critical thinking is essential when consuming media. This involves questioning the information presented: Who is the source? What might be their motive for presenting the information in this way? Is the information supported by evidence? Are there alternative perspectives that are not being presented? By engaging in this level of analysis, individuals can better assess the credibility of the information and avoid taking it at face value.

Another aspect of ethical information consumption is the differentiation between facts and opinions. News reports should ideally present factual information and clearly distinguish it from opinion or analysis. As consumers, recognizing these differences helps us to form more informed and nuanced opinions ourselves.

Digital literacy also plays a crucial role in navigating media truth ethically. In the age of the internet, where anyone can publish content, digital literacy involves the skills required to search, evaluate, and contribute information online responsibly. This means being aware of the credibility of online sources and understanding how to verify information through reputable fact-checking organizations or by cross-referencing multiple reliable sources.

Ethical media consumption also involves a proactive approach to combating misinformation. This can mean reporting or flagging false information when encountered online, discussing media ethics with peers, or even engaging in forums to promote factual discourse. By taking these actions, individuals contribute to a more truth-oriented media landscape.

Moreover, supporting ethical journalism is another way to navigate media truth. This can be done by subscribing to news outlets known for high journalistic standards, supporting non-profit journalism organizations, and consuming a variety of news sources to get a comprehensive view of the news landscape. Financial support helps maintain the independence of media outlets, allowing them to produce in-depth, researched journalism without undue reliance on advertising revenue or external influences.

The responsibilities of media professionals are equally crucial in navigating truth in media. Journalists and media outlets must strive to uphold the highest ethical standards in their reporting. This includes fact-checking, revising content for accuracy before publication, providing balanced views, and correcting any errors promptly and transparently.

Navigating truth in the media is a joint responsibility between media producers and consumers. By understanding and practicing ethical information consumption and supporting responsible journalism, individuals can help foster a media environment that values and prioritizes truth. This ethical approach not only enhances personal knowledge and understanding but also contributes to the overall health of a democratic society.

"In matters of health, ethical choices are not just
about personal well-being but about ensuring
equitable access to care and promoting the dignity
of every individual."

CHAPTER FOURTEEN

Financial Ethics: Responsibility with Money and Resources

Financial ethics encompasses the values and principles that govern our behaviors and decisions regarding money and resources. It touches on various aspects of life, including personal finance, business operations, and economic policies.

Ethical financial management is crucial not only for ensuring personal and organizational prosperity but also for promoting fairness and sustainability within the broader community and economy. Responsible financial behavior reflects a commitment to honesty, integrity, and accountability, values that are essential in fostering trust and stability in economic transactions.

Personal Financial Ethics

At the personal level, financial ethics involves managing one's finances in ways that are honest and fair. This includes adhering to laws and regulations regarding taxes and reporting income accurately. It also means avoiding deceitful behaviors such as fraud or theft, which undermine the trust on which economic systems rely.

Ethical personal finance also involves considering the broader impact of one's financial decisions. For example, choosing to invest in companies that prioritize sustainability and ethical business practices can contribute to positive social and environmental outcomes. Similarly, choosing products and services from businesses that treat their employees well and operate fairly supports the proliferation of ethical business practices.

Budgeting and Debt Management

Responsible financial management includes maintaining a realistic budget that accounts for income and expenses, ensuring that spending does not exceed what one can afford. This approach not only prevents personal financial crises but also reduces the risk of contributing to broader economic instability.

Debt management is another critical aspect of financial ethics. While borrowing is often necessary, it should be approached with caution and responsibility. This means understanding the terms of debt, ensuring the ability to repay it, and considering the implications of taking on debt for oneself and for lenders.

Ethics in Business Finance

In the business context, financial ethics involves transparent financial reporting and fair financial practices that do not mislead shareholders, customers, or the public. This includes providing accurate financial disclosures and avoiding practices like embezzlement or using insider information for personal gain.

Fairness in pricing, paying wages, and contracting also falls under the umbrella of business financial ethics. Businesses have a responsibility to set prices that are fair and reflect the true cost of production, including paying fair wages to employees. Ethical businesses also honor their contractual obligations and engage in fair negotiation practices that do not exploit partners or suppliers.

Corporate Social Responsibility

Corporate social responsibility (CSR) is an important component of financial ethics at the organizational level. CSR involves companies taking responsibility for the social and environmental impacts of their operations. This includes efforts like investing in community development, reducing environmental footprints, and ensuring sustainable resource management. By adhering to CSR principles, businesses demonstrate their commitment to ethical financial practices that extend beyond profit maximization.

Economic Policies and Global Finance

On a larger scale, financial ethics involves advocating for and implementing economic policies that promote fairness, economic equality, and sustainability. This includes policies that prevent exploitative practices, regulate financial markets to avoid undue risks, and manage public resources responsibly.

Ethical challenges in global finance, such as tax evasion, money laundering, and exploitation of labor, require international cooperation and stringent regulations to address effectively. Promoting transparency and accountability at the global level helps ensure that financial systems contribute positively to society and do not perpetuate inequality or environmental degradation.

Financial ethics is a multifaceted field that encompasses personal behavior, business practices, and economic policies. By embracing financial ethics, individuals and organizations can contribute to a more just and stable economic system. Ethical financial practices ensure that resources are used responsibly, risks are managed carefully, and the broader social and environmental impacts of financial decisions are considered. Ultimately, financial ethics is about making choices that respect and enhance the well-being of all stakeholders involved, ensuring that our financial systems serve the common good and foster sustainable prosperity.

"Ethical education is the foundation upon which a just and compassionate society is built, shaping the moral compass of future generations."

CHAPTER FIFTEEN

Health and Ethics: Making Moral Choices in Health and Wellness

Health and wellness are fundamental aspects of life, influencing not just individual well-being but also the broader societal fabric. Ethical considerations in health encompass a wide range of issues, from personal lifestyle choices to global healthcare policies.

The Foundation of Health Ethics

Health ethics is grounded in principles such as autonomy, beneficence, non-maleficence, and justice. These principles guide decisions in healthcare by ensuring that actions are taken in the best interest of patients without causing harm, respecting individual choices, and distributing healthcare resources fairly.

Personal Health Choices

On a personal level, making ethical decisions about one's health involves considering the impacts of lifestyle choices not only on oneself but also on others. For example, choosing to smoke may affect not just the smoker's health but also the health of those around them through secondhand smoke. Ethically, individuals should aim to make health decisions that do not adversely affect others, such as maintaining a healthy lifestyle, getting vaccinated to prevent the spread of diseases, and using healthcare resources responsibly.

Confidentiality and Privacy

Confidentiality is a core ethical principle in healthcare. Patients trust health professionals with sensitive personal information that should be protected to maintain privacy and dignity. Breaching confidentiality without just cause can damage the patient-provider relationship and undermine the trust that is essential for effective healthcare delivery.

Consent in Healthcare

Informed consent is another fundamental ethical issue. Patients have the right to be fully informed about their treatment options and to make decisions about their care without coercion. This includes understanding the risks, benefits, and alternatives to proposed treatments. Health professionals must ensure that consent is obtained ethically, respecting patient autonomy and providing all necessary information for informed decision-making.

Healthcare Access and Equity

At the societal level, ethical issues in health often revolve around access to care and the equitable distribution of healthcare resources. In many places, not everyone has the same access to healthcare due to economic disparities, geographic locations, or systemic biases. Ethically, society should strive to minimize these disparities and work towards healthcare equity, ensuring that all individuals have access to the care they need.

Global Health Ethics

Global health ethics deals with health issues that transcend national boundaries, such as pandemics, access to essential medicines, and international health disparities. Ethical challenges in this realm include deciding how to allocate limited resources during a crisis, addressing the health needs of refugees and displaced populations, and managing the pricing and distribution of life-saving medications worldwide.

Ethical Research and Innovation

The realm of medical research and technological innovation also presents significant ethical challenges. The development of new treatments and medical technologies must be guided by ethical research practices. This includes ensuring that clinical trials are conducted responsibly, participants are treated ethically, and the benefits of innovations are accessible to all, not just a privileged few.

End-of-Life Care

End-of-life care is a particularly sensitive area of health ethics. Decisions about withholding or withdrawing life-sustaining treatment involve deep ethical considerations about the value of life, the quality of life, and the rights of patients and families. These decisions must be approached with compassion, respect for the patient's wishes, and careful ethical reasoning.

Ethical considerations in health and wellness are essential for fostering a society that values well-being, fairness, and respect for individual choices. By adhering to ethical principles in personal health behaviors, healthcare practice, and policy-making, we can ensure that health-related decisions promote not only physical well-being but also moral integrity and social justice. Making moral choices in health and wellness not only benefits individuals but also strengthens the collective health of communities and the ethical fabric of society. Through informed, compassionate, and ethical decision-making, we can navigate the complex health challenges of today and tomorrow, ensuring that all individuals receive the care and respect they deserve.

"Art has the power to transcend boundaries, speaking to the soul and expressing the values that bind us together as human beings."

CHAPTER SIXTEEN

Ethical Education: Teaching Values from Childhood to Adulthood

Ethical education is fundamental to developing individuals who are capable of making informed, responsible choices throughout their lives. This form of education spans from childhood to adulthood, embedding values that are essential for personal development, professional integrity, and civic responsibility.

The Role of Ethical Education

Ethical education aims to instill core values such as honesty, respect, fairness, and compassion. These values are critical in navigating the complexities of social interactions and professional responsibilities. Furthermore, ethical education fosters critical thinking and moral reasoning, enabling individuals to apply ethical principles to various life situations.

Ethical Education in Early Childhood

The foundation of ethical education begins in early childhood. Young children are highly impressionable and learn values primarily through observation and imitation. Parents and early educators play a crucial role by modeling ethical behaviors and making values like sharing, kindness, and honesty part of daily interactions. Storytelling and role-playing can be effective techniques at this stage, as they allow children to explore ethical concepts in a relatable and engaging way.

Primary and Secondary Education

As children grow, ethical education becomes more structured and integrated into the school curriculum. Schools have the responsibility to create environments that promote respect and inclusivity while actively teaching ethical decision-making. This can be achieved through classroom discussions, ethical dilemma exercises, and service-learning projects that allow students to practice applying values in real-world contexts. Teachers are instrumental in guiding these discussions and helping students develop a nuanced understanding of ethical issues.

Higher Education and Beyond

In higher education, ethical education often becomes more specialized, reflecting the complexities of adult life and professional fields. Universities and colleges have the opportunity to deepen students' understanding of ethics within specific disciplines, such as business ethics, medical ethics, or engineering ethics. This specialized approach helps prepare students for the ethical challenges they may face in their careers, equipping them with the tools to make decisions that are not only effective but also morally sound.

Lifelong Learning of Ethics

Ethical education does not end with formal schooling; it is a lifelong process. Adults continue to face new ethical dilemmas and situations that require moral reasoning. Continuing education courses, workshops, and seminars play an important role in this ongoing education, providing opportunities for individuals to refresh their understanding and engage with new ethical challenges as they arise in society.

Challenges in Ethical Education

One of the challenges in ethical education is ensuring that it is relevant and resonant with diverse student populations. Educators must consider cultural, socioeconomic, and personal backgrounds when designing and implementing ethical education programs. Additionally, the increasing influence of technology and globalization presents new ethical issues that education systems must address proactively.

Strategies for Effective Ethical Education

Effective ethical education relies on active and engaged learning methods that encourage students to think critically and reflect on their values. Strategies include:

Case Studies: Analyzing real-life scenarios helps students apply ethical theories and principles in a practical context.

Debates and Discussions: These foster critical thinking and allow students to explore different perspectives, enhancing their ability to navigate complex ethical issues.

Community Engagement: Participating in community service provides practical experiences that bring ethical lessons to life.

Reflective Writing: Journals or essays on ethical topics encourage personal reflection, helping students internalize ethical concepts.

Ethical education is essential for nurturing individuals who can contribute positively to society. By teaching values from childhood to adulthood, we equip individuals with the tools necessary to make ethical decisions throughout their lives. Effective ethical education not only promotes individual morality but also cultivates a more just, compassionate, and ethical society. As we continue to face new and complex ethical challenges, the importance of ongoing ethical education becomes ever more apparent, underscoring the need for a committed and nuanced approach to teaching values across the lifespan.

"*Political integrity is the bedrock of a healthy democracy, built upon the pillars of transparency, accountability, and the common good.*"

CHAPTER SEVENTEEN

Art and Ethics: Expressing Values Through Creativity

Art is a powerful medium for expressing ideas, emotions, and values. It transcends cultural and linguistic barriers, delivering messages that can influence thoughts and provoke discussion. Here, I will explain the intersection of art and ethics, examining how art can serve as a vehicle for expressing and reflecting upon ethical values, and the responsibilities artists have in relation to their creations and audiences.

The Role of Art in Society

Art plays a multifaceted role in society. It is not only a source of aesthetic pleasure but also a form of communication that can challenge societal norms, highlight injustices, and inspire change. Through various forms—painting, sculpture, literature, film, and music—artists have the unique ability to comment on moral issues, raise ethical questions, and encourage viewers or readers to reflect on their own beliefs and behaviors.

Art as a Reflection of Ethical Values

Many artists use their work to explore and express ethical values such as justice, equality, freedom, and respect for life. For instance, a painter might create works that highlight the struggles of marginalized communities, or a filmmaker might produce documentaries that explore the ethical implications of environmental conservation. These creations often aim to spark ethical reflection and motivate audiences to consider deeper moral issues that they might not engage with in everyday life.

The Ethical Responsibility of Artists

While art is a platform for free expression, artists also face ethical considerations regarding the impact of their work. This raises questions about the responsibilities artists have to their subjects and their audiences. For example, when dealing with sensitive subjects such as trauma or injustice, artists must navigate the fine line between representation and exploitation. Ethical art respects the dignity and integrity of its subjects, avoiding sensationalism or trivialization of serious issues.

Moreover, artists must consider the potential consequences of their work. Art that aims to provoke or challenge may also offend or cause harm, intentionally or unintentionally. Artists need to balance their creative ambitions with an awareness of their audience's diverse perspectives and potential vulnerabilities. This doesn't mean censoring creativity but rather considering the broader impacts of their work and striving to engage responsibly with their audience.

Art, Censorship, and Freedom of Expression

A central ethical issue in the arts is the tension between freedom of expression and the potential harm that art can cause. Censorship can be seen as a restriction on artistic freedom, yet, unchecked freedom can lead to the dissemination of harmful stereotypes or hateful ideologies. Ethical art navigates these waters carefully, aiming to uphold the value of freedom of expression while being mindful of not perpetuating harm.

Artistic Authenticity

Another ethical concern in the arts is authenticity, which involves being true to one's artistic vision and not compromising one's values for commercial success or popular approval. This includes issues of artistic theft or plagiarism, where the ethical principles of honesty and respect for the original creator's intellectual property are at stake. Artists face the challenge of creating original work that respects the contributions of others while also adding something uniquely their own.

The Ethical Consumption of Art

Ethical considerations also extend to consumers of art. Audiences have the responsibility to engage with art thoughtfully, respecting the creator's intent while also critically assessing the messages conveyed. Ethical consumption of art involves recognizing the influence of art on our perceptions and attitudes and taking care to support works that align with ethical principles.

Art and ethics are deeply intertwined. Through their creative expressions, artists have the power to influence society, shape cultural norms, and provoke ethical reflection. By considering the ethical dimensions of their work, artists contribute not only to the aesthetic landscape but also to the moral discourse of society. As consumers of art, we also play a role in this dynamic by choosing what to support and how we let art influence us. Together, through the creation and consumption of art, we can foster a more thoughtful, ethical, and expressive society.

"Spiritual wisdom reminds us that ethical living is not just about following rules; it's about embodying love, compassion, and kindness in every thought, word, and deed."

CHAPTER EIGHTEEN

Political Integrity: Ethics in Governance and Citizenship

Political integrity is a cornerstone of effective governance and a thriving democratic society. It involves the adherence to moral principles by government officials, politicians, and citizens alike, ensuring that public affairs are conducted honestly, transparently, and for the common good.

The Essence of Political Integrity

Political integrity requires that all actions within the sphere of governance be guided by ethics. This includes adherence to laws, fair treatment of all citizens, transparency in decision-making, and accountability for actions. Without these elements, trust in government deteriorates, leading to cynicism, apathy, or even unrest among the populace.

Ethics in Governance

At the heart of ethical governance is the commitment to serve the public interest above personal or party interests. This commitment should be evident in all aspects of governance, from policy-making and public spending to electoral processes and international relations.

One of the primary ethical challenges in governance is corruption, which can manifest in various forms such as bribery, nepotism, and embezzlement. Combating corruption requires robust systems of law enforcement and judicial oversight, but also a culture of integrity that starts at the highest levels of government. Leaders must model the ethical behavior they expect to see, creating an environment where unethical actions are neither tolerated nor excused.

Transparency is another critical aspect of ethical governance. Citizens must be able to see and understand the processes by which decisions are made on their behalf. This transparency is achieved through open meetings, public records, and freedom of information. When governments operate openly, they are more likely to act in the public interest and less likely to engage in unethical behavior.

Accountability is closely tied to transparency. Officials must be held accountable for their actions, especially when those actions deviate from ethical standards. Mechanisms for accountability include checks and balances within government, independent auditing bodies, and a free press that is able to investigate and report on government activity without fear of censorship or retaliation.

Ethics in Citizenship

While much focus is placed on the responsibilities of those who hold office, citizens themselves play a crucial role in maintaining political integrity. Ethical citizenship involves staying informed about public issues, participating in the democratic process, and holding one's representatives accountable.

Informed citizens are better equipped to make wise decisions about whom to vote for and what policies to support. This means taking the time to understand the issues, knowing where candidates stand on those issues, and discerning the difference between factual reporting and misinformation.

Voting is perhaps the most fundamental aspect of ethical citizenship. By participating in elections, citizens exercise their right to influence government and its policies. Ethical voting means making choices based on careful consideration of the common good, rather than personal gain or narrow group interests.

Beyond voting, ethical citizenship can include other forms of participation such as attending town hall meetings, joining community boards, or volunteering for local initiatives. Active involvement gives citizens a voice in their government and helps ensure that their interests are represented.

Citizens also have a duty to hold government accountable. This can be done through peaceful protest, petitioning for change, or simply speaking out against unethical behavior in government. When citizens are engaged and vigilant, they serve as a powerful check on the potential abuses of power.

Political integrity is essential for the health and sustainability of any democracy. It requires commitment not only from those in positions of power but also from the citizenry they serve. By prioritizing ethics in governance and citizenship, we foster a political environment that is fair, transparent, and accountable, ensuring that government truly serves the public interest. Ethical governance and active citizenship create a virtuous cycle that strengthens the fabric of society and promotes the well-being of all its members.

"Towards an ethical future, we must envision a world where every individual is empowered to live with integrity, creating a ripple effect of positive change that spans generations."

CHAPTER NINETEEN

Spiritual Dimensions of Ethics: Exploring Moral Frameworks Across Cultures

Ethics, the discipline that deals with what is morally good and bad, right and wrong, extends beyond secular realms into spiritual and religious contexts. Across cultures, religious and spiritual traditions provide frameworks that guide followers in making ethical decisions and leading moral lives.

The Role of Religion in Shaping Ethics

Religion often plays a central role in defining ethical norms within a society. Many of the world's religions, including Christianity, Islam, Hinduism, Buddhism, and Judaism, have established detailed moral frameworks that guide the behavior of their adherents. These frameworks are usually rooted in sacred texts, religious doctrines, and the teachings of spiritual leaders.

For example, in Christianity, the Ten Commandments are a set of ethical guidelines that many Christians use to guide their decisions. Similarly, in Islam, the Quran provides a comprehensive code of conduct that includes guidelines on everything from family life to business dealings. In Hinduism, concepts like Dharma (duty, righteousness) guide individuals on how to live virtuously according to their role and stage of life.

Common Ethical Themes Across Religions

Despite the diversity of religious beliefs, there are common ethical themes that appear across different spiritual traditions. These include the principles of compassion, honesty, justice, and respect for life. For instance:

Compassion is emphasized in Buddhism's teachings on loving-kindness and in the Christian practice of charity.

Honesty is upheld in the Islamic tradition through prohibitions against lying and in the Jewish commandment against bearing false witness.

Justice is a central theme in the social teachings of the Catholic Church and in the Hindu laws of karma, which assert that every action has consequences.

Respect for life is evident in the Jain practice of ahimsa (non-violence) and in the Buddhist precept to refrain from taking life.

These commonalities suggest that while religions may differ in their rituals and beliefs, they often share similar ethical goals and values, promoting behaviors that enhance the well-being of individuals and communities.

Ethics and Personal Spirituality

Aside from organized religion, personal spirituality also influences ethical perspectives and behaviors. Many people derive their sense of right and wrong from their personal spiritual experiences and beliefs, even if these are not aligned with any formal religious doctrine.

Personal spirituality often emphasizes inner peace, personal integrity, and a harmonious relationship with others and the environment. It encourages individuals to look within themselves to find ethical guidance and to act in ways that reflect their deepest values and beliefs.

Cultural Variations in Ethical Perceptions

While there are universal ethical themes, the interpretation and application of these themes can vary significantly across different cultures. What is considered ethical in one cultural context may be viewed differently in another, based on historical, social, and environmental factors.

For example, the concept of family loyalty plays a significant role in many Asian cultures, influencing business practices and personal decisions in ways that might be considered nepotism or a conflict of interest in Western contexts. Similarly, the value placed on community welfare over individual rights in many African and Indigenous cultures can lead to ethical decisions that prioritize group benefits over individual freedoms.

Navigating Ethical Diversity

In today's globalized world, understanding and respecting the diversity of ethical frameworks across cultures and religions is crucial. This does not mean abandoning one's own ethical principles but rather developing an awareness of and respect for different ethical perspectives. It involves engaging in dialogue, sharing values, and learning from each other's moral traditions.

The spiritual dimensions of ethics enrich our understanding of morality by connecting it with the deeper values and beliefs that define human cultures and spiritual traditions. Exploring these dimensions across different religions and cultures not only highlights the diversity of ethical thought but also the common moral ground shared by humanity. By appreciating the spiritual foundations of ethics, we can foster a more inclusive, respectful, and compassionate global community, better equipped to address the complex moral challenges of the modern world.

"*The journey towards ethical enlightenment
begins with a single step—one guided by the light
of conscience and the courage to do what is right,
even when it is difficult.*"

CHAPTER TWENTY

Towards an Ethical Future: Envisioning and Creating a Better World

In today's rapidly changing world, the pursuit of an ethical future is more important than ever. As we face global challenges like environmental degradation, social inequality, and technological disruption, the need for a strong ethical foundation across all aspects of society cannot be overstated.

Defining an Ethical Future

An ethical future is one in which fairness, justice, compassion, and sustainability are not just ideals, but realities embedded in everyday practices at individual, community, and global levels. This future involves a world where individuals not only pursue their own good but also consider the well-being of others, including those in distant places and future generations who will inherit the results of today's decisions.

Ethical Considerations in a Globalized World

In a globalized world, our actions can have far-reaching impacts. Ethical global citizenship requires us to think about how our lifestyles, consumption patterns, and business practices affect people and environments worldwide. For instance, buying clothes produced in factories with poor working conditions or using technology that contributes to significant e-waste can perpetuate cycles of harm and exploitation. Thus, an ethical future involves making choices that promote sustainability, equity, and respect for human dignity across the globe.

Technological Advancements and Ethics

As technology continues to advance, it brings both opportunities and ethical challenges. Issues such as data privacy, surveillance, artificial intelligence, and the potential for job displacement due to automation require us to think critically about how these technologies are developed and used. An ethical future involves creating technologies that enhance the quality of life without infringing on rights and freedoms, and that consider the long-term impacts on society and the environment.

Environmental Sustainability

One of the most pressing issues of our time is environmental sustainability. An ethical future is not possible without a commitment to practices that protect and preserve the Earth. This means moving towards renewable energy sources, reducing waste, protecting biodiversity, and adopting policies that mitigate the effects of climate change. It also involves educating and empowering citizens to make environmentally responsible choices and to advocate for policies that ensure a healthy planet.

Social Justice and Inclusivity

Creating an ethical future also requires addressing inequalities and ensuring that everyone, regardless of background, has the opportunity to live a fulfilling life. This includes tackling issues like poverty, discrimination, and access to education and healthcare. It means advocating for policies that promote social justice and provide support to those who are most vulnerable. Additionally, it involves fostering an inclusive culture that values diversity and the contributions of all members of society.

Ethical Leadership

Leadership plays a crucial role in shaping the ethical standards of organizations and governments. Ethical leaders are those who act with integrity, transparency, and a commitment to the public good. They inspire others by example and create environments where ethical practices are the norm, not the exception. Encouraging ethical leadership involves training and systems that promote ethical decision-making at all levels of society.

Public Engagement and Responsibility

A key component of creating an ethical future is active engagement by the public. This means that individuals not only stay informed about the ethical issues affecting their communities and the world but also take action to promote ethical outcomes. Voting, volunteering, participating in community discussions, and advocating for change are all ways that individuals can contribute to a more ethical society.

Envisioning and creating an ethical future is a dynamic and ongoing process that requires the commitment of individuals, communities, businesses, and governments. It involves examining the impact of our actions on others and the planet, making informed choices, and advocating for policies and practices that promote fairness, justice, and sustainability. By embedding ethical considerations into every aspect of our lives, we can work towards a future that is not only prosperous but also compassionate and just. This future is within our reach if we choose to act with the collective good in mind, fostering a world where ethical principles guide us toward a brighter, more equitable tomorrow.

"In the tapestry of life, each ethical choice we make adds a vibrant thread, weaving together a masterpiece of compassion, justice, and integrity that enriches the world for generations to come."

CHAPTER TWENTY-ONE

Summary

This Book serves as a comprehensive guide for navigating the complex ethical dilemmas of modern life. This book provides insights and practical advice on how individuals can develop personal integrity and contribute positively to society by embracing ethical principles.

1. The Foundation of Integrity: Understanding Core Ethical Values This opening chapter sets the stage by exploring the foundational values that underpin a life of integrity, such as honesty, respect, and responsibility. It emphasizes the importance of consistency between one's actions and beliefs and the role of self-reflection in maintaining personal integrity.

2. Empathy in Action: Cultivating Compassion in Everyday Life Empathy is discussed as a crucial element of ethical living. This chapter highlights how understanding and sharing the feelings of others can lead to more compassionate and considerate interactions, enhancing personal relationships and community bonds.

3. Decisions at the Crossroads: Navigating Personal Ethical Dilemmas Readers are guided through strategies for making tough ethical decisions. The chapter emphasizes the importance of weighing potential outcomes and staying true to one's moral principles when faced with challenging choices.

4. The Ethics of Relationships: Honesty and Trust in Personal Connections Exploring ethical dynamics within relationships, this chapter underscores the significance of honesty and trust in building and maintaining healthy personal connections, outlining how these elements foster deeper mutual understanding and respect.

5. Global Citizenship: The Ethics of Living in a Connected World Focusing on the global implications of our actions, this chapter encourages readers to consider their impact on the wider world and highlights the importance of acting as responsible global citizens in an interconnected society.

6. Ethical Consumption: Making Responsible Choices as a Consumer The ethical dimensions of consumer choices are examined here, urging readers to consider the social and environmental impacts of their purchasing decisions and to support businesses that adhere to ethical practices.

7. Sustainability and Ethics: Protecting Our Planet for Future Generations This chapter delves into the importance of sustainability, discussing how ethical considerations regarding environmental protection and resource management can ensure a livable world for future generations.

8. The Power of Community: Building Supportive Ethical Networks The role of community in fostering ethical behavior is emphasized, highlighting how supportive networks can enhance personal growth and promote collective well-being.

9. Workplace Integrity: Ethics in Professional Environments Readers are encouraged to apply ethical principles in their professional lives, focusing on fairness, accountability, and respect in the workplace to create a positive and productive work environment.

10. Digital Dilemmas: Ethics in the Age of Technology This chapter addresses the ethical challenges presented by digital technology, including issues of privacy, misinformation, and the responsible use of online platforms.

11. Ethical Leadership: Inspiring Integrity in Others The qualities of ethical leadership are explored, demonstrating how leaders can inspire integrity and foster ethical cultures within their organizations and communities.

12. Conflict and Resolution: Ethical Approaches to Disagreements Strategies for resolving conflicts ethically are discussed, with an emphasis on understanding, fairness, and respectful communication as tools for finding mutually beneficial solutions.

13. The Ethics of Information: Navigating Truth in the Media This chapter encourages critical engagement with media, advocating for the responsible consumption and distribution of information and emphasizing the importance of discerning truth in the digital age.

14. Financial Ethics: Responsibility with Money and Resources The ethical aspects of financial management are outlined, urging individuals and organizations to handle financial resources with honesty, transparency, and consideration for the broader economic impact.

15. Health and Ethics: Making Moral Choices in Health and Wellness Health-related ethical issues are examined, including the importance of informed consent, confidentiality, and equitable access to healthcare services.

16. Ethical Education: Teaching Values from Childhood to

Adulthood The importance of instilling ethical values from an early age is discussed, highlighting education's role in shaping morally conscious individuals.

17. Art and Ethics: Expressing Values Through Creativity The relationship between art and ethics is explored, considering how artistic expression can reflect and promote ethical considerations and societal values.

18. Political Integrity: Ethics in Governance and Citizenship This chapter discusses the critical role of ethics in governance and the responsibilities of both leaders and citizens in maintaining a just and effective political system.

19. Spiritual Dimensions of Ethics: Exploring Moral Frameworks Across Cultures Different religious and cultural perspectives on ethics are examined, showing how various spiritual beliefs can influence moral behavior and ethical decision-making.

20. Towards an Ethical Future: Envisioning and Creating a Better World The final chapter synthesizes the themes discussed throughout the book, envisioning a future where ethical practices are integrated into all aspects of life, leading to a more just, sustainable, and compassionate world.

Throughout the book, emphasizes the interconnectedness of individual actions and broader societal issues, urging readers to actively engage in ethical thought and behavior in all areas of life. The book serves as a practical guide for anyone seeking to understand and apply ethical principles in a complex world, encouraging a shift towards more thoughtful and responsible living.

Citation And References

This book represents the culmination of extensive research and meticulous analysis, incorporating a diverse range of sources, including numerous books, scholarly studies, and personal experiences. Additionally, I have scoured various websites to gather relevant information and data essential for the compilation of this work. I have taken every precaution to ensure the accuracy of the information presented and have diligently cited all sources to acknowledge their contributions.

Despite these efforts, the possibility of inadvertent errors remains. I deeply value the insights of my readers and appreciate any feedback that can help identify and rectify such inaccuracies. I encourage you to bring any discrepancies to my attention.

Your feedback is not only welcome but crucial, as it will aid in correcting current editions and enhancing the content of future ones. I am committed to maintaining the highest standards of accuracy and reliability in my work and thank you for your support and understanding.

Additionally, I firmly uphold the principle of freedom of speech and expression as guaranteed under Article 19(1)(a) of the Constitution of India, and I respect the diverse viewpoints and expressions of all readers.

Other Books Of The Author

1. Empowering Minds: A Journey into Women's Self-Discovery and Power
2. The Dynamics of Motivation: Catalyzing Thought into Action
3. Meditative Minds: The Path to Inner Peace and Clarity
4. The Psychology of Child Education: Nurturing Future Generations
5. Ethical Enlightenment: A Modern Guide to Living with Integrity
6. Voices of Empowerment: Stories of Women Rising Against Odds
7. Social Psychology in Everyday Life: Understanding Human Connections
8. The Essence of Motivational Speaking: Inspiring Change in Others
9. Balancing Acts: Women, Work, and the Will to Lead
10. Mindful Parenting: Raising Children with Compassion and Awareness
11. The Power of Positive Aging: Embracing Life After Fifty
12. Building Resilient Communities: Social Work in Action
13. The Ethical Educator: Principles for Teaching and Learning
14. From Insight to Impact: Social Psychology for a Better World
15. Cultivating Compassion: A Guide to Ethical Living
16. The Science of Self-Help: Navigating Life's Challenges with Psychological Wisdom
17. The Mindful Leader: Meditation Techniques for Modern Management
18. Breaking Barriers: Women's Pathways to Leadership and Empowerment
19. Educating Hearts: The Role of Emotional Intelligence in Child Development
20. Transformative Talks: Insights into Motivational Oratory
21. Green Ethics: A Path to Sustainable Living
22. Soul Ethics: Finding Spirituality Through Moral Living

Contact

Dr. Minakshi Bansal
Social Activist
Ahmedabad, Gujarat, Bharat
minakshiindiag20@yahoo.com

|| LOKAHA SAMASTHAHA SUKHINO BHAVANTU ||

• 131 •